Memoir of the Rev. Francis Higginson
by Joseph Barlow Felt

Copyright © 2019 by HardPress

Address:
HardPress
8345 NW 66TH ST #2561
MIAMI FL 33166-2626
USA
Email: info@hardpress.net

US
12708
1.5

elt - Francis Higginson. 1852.

US 12768.1.5

HARVARD COLLEGE LIBRARY

THE BEQUEST OF

EVERT JANSEN WENDELL
(CLASS OF 1882)
OF NEW YORK

1918

MEMOIR

OF THE

REV. FRANCIS HIGGINSON.

MEMOIR

OF THE

REV. FRANCIS HIGGINSON

BY JOSEPH B. FELT.

The righteous shall be in everlasting remembrance.....*Psalms*.
Dignum laude virum musa vetat mori.....*Horace*.

BOSTON:
THOMAS PRINCE, PRINTER, 11 1-2 TREMONT ROW,
Office of the N. E. Hist. and Gen. Register.
1852.

CORRECTIONS AND EXPLANATIONS.

Page 2, line 24, for *Heldersham* read *Hildersham*.—P. 4, l. 24, omit *before all* between *sin* and *rebuke*.—P. 10, l. 26, Asylum should have but one *s*.—P. 10, l. 40, two ships, besides the three, were to sail about three weeks after.—P. 20, line 14, for *goodly* read *godly*.—P. 20, l. 21, supply *hereby* between *may* and *be*.—P. 20, l. 31, for *John* read *Thomas* Goff.—P. 23, l. 17, omit *the* before March.

MEMOIR

OF THE

REV. FRANCIS HIGGINSON.

BY JOSEPH B. FELT.

Wise, emphatically wise, is the government of the universe. While the christian philanthropist ventures his all in the cause of reformation, and knows not that his eye will ever behold the end, for which he toils, he cherishes a heartfelt assurance, that a reward awaits him above the skies, proportioned to the purity of his motives and the fulness of his sacrifices. This is the key, which unlocks the mystery as to the readiness, with which multitudes of our race have forsaken the dearest attractions of life, and subjected themselves to labor, peril and suffering. This explains the reasonableness of the holy enterprize, in which Francis Higginson and his associates embarked, not knowing what of earthly experience awaited them. But this they knew, and it was the impulse above all others, that the God whom they trusted and whom they served, would not suffer an iota of their devotedness to him and his cause, though hidden from the eye of human perception in its exercise and result, to be lost in his assignment of their everlasting portion.

Connecting the short period of Mr. Higginson's continuance at Naumkeag, with that he passed in his father-land, we will endeavor to follow him by the comparatively small number of points in his history, which the consuming progress of time has left to our vision. He was the son of John Higginson,[1] born 1587. He received his A. B. 1609, at Jesus College, and his A. M. 1613, at St. John's, both of Cambridge University. We are informed, that he was settled as a strict conformist, with the rites and ceremonies of the national church, about 1615, at Claybrooke,[2] one of the parishes in Leicester.

---

[1] There is a tradition among one branch of the Higginson family in England, that this person was drowned in returning from a place where he had preached, at the advanced age of 104. It seems not probable as to the great age, though possible.

[2] Claybrooke parish, in the census of England and Wales, 1841, is stated to be in the counties of Leicester and Warwick.

Giving full proof, that he felt the importance of being a herald of the gospel, his precept and example deeply impressed his people, that his supreme desire and endeavor were to secure their spiritual, more than their temporal good, though benevolence shone out from all his labors for the whole circle of their best interests. "The main scope of his ministry," as Cotton Mather[1] observed, "was to promote first, a thorough conversion, and then a godly conversation among" them. In addition to this, his manners were courteous and obliging, his oratory, attainments and talents superior. Crowds, from the neighborhood, came to hear his dispensations of divine truth. His efforts were not in vain. As the reward, most precious to his heart, the Spirit of grace rendered them the means of turning many from darkness to light. Thus being, in his course, like the sun in its constant revolutions, a source of benefit to all within his influence, he kept his engagement of close conformity with Ecclesiastical rules, for a considerable number of years.

The question of such compliance was receiving increased attention and discussion, from no small number of the choicest clergy. While on the one hand, there were the favor and encouragement of the State, to hold by its spiritual appointments, there were, on the other, its frowns and prosecutions for turning to an opposite direction. Being drawn, by kindred sympathies and motives, to the society of Heldersham and Hooker, he was induced more fully to search the Scriptures, so that he might ascertain whether the charge, that corruptions, in doctrine and practice, had alarmingly crept into the established Church, was true. The result was, that, about 1627, he took a decided stand with the Puritans. A consequence of such committal and of his own practical regard for consistency, was his exclusion from the parish, for whom he had faithfully toiled, as answerable to a tribunal, infinitely higher than human.

Though aware, that he was numbered with the advocates for reform, then an odious distinction with their opponents, the large congregation, who still waited on his ministrations, could not consent to relinquish them. "He was unto them as a very lovely song of one, that hath a pleasant voice, and can play well on an instrument." They obtained permission for him to preach for them a part of the Sabbath, and, on the other, to assist an aged clergyman, who needed his help. His hearers freely contributed towards the support of himself and family. While they so manifested their attachment to him, the other clergymen of the Town invited him, until they were forbidden, to officiate in their churches. By this means "he preached successively in three" of these sanctuaries, even after he was legally disqualified by his non-conformity.

Besides the labors already mentioned, he dispensed the truths of inspiration to a people at Belgrave village, a mile from Leicester. The calls for his service, were numerous, and he heard them with gladness of heart. It would have been pleasant to him, beyond

---

[1] From the Magnalia of this learned author, many facts of this memoir are taken.

all the contributions of earthly greatness, could he have so pursued and finished his temporal career. But he had already been tolerated by Bishop Williams of Lincoln, whose diocese included Leicester, more than many high churchmen approved, and his liberty was to come under the control of Bishop Laud, who felt that his administration of office should be less indulgent. When this prelate had a difference with the former, he pursued the Puritans, who were favored by him, with severity, supposing that his obligation to the kingdom could be sooner and better discharged in this manner, than otherwise. But such policy brought fear and desolation to many a happy fireside, consecrated to the cause of Christ. Thus it was soon to be with the home of Higginson. The dread of displeased authority was to imbitter its joys, and the threats of the Star Chamber to scatter its happy inmates.

Before, however, the storm began to beat in all its severity, some incidents occurred illustrative of Mr. Higginson's faithful and forgiving deportment. Among the evils, which he endeavored to remove from his people, according to the Thirty-nine Articles, was the allowance of immoral persons to be partakers of the Lord's supper. When the elements of this sacred festival were to be administered, he preached from the words, "Give not that which is holy to the dogs." Beginning to distribute the bread, an intemperate man, who failed to comply with his instruction, advanced for his portion. Mr. Higginson, in accordance with the Rubric, observed to him, that he was unwilling to grant him the privilege until he should manifest evidence of repentance. The individual so reproved, left the church much displeased. He lived but a little while after, and died with the words of despair on his lips.

Another, a gentleman who lived in an adjacent parish, was greatly offended because his wife frequently attended the preaching of Mr. Higginson, and declared that he would be revenged on him. He, therefore, prepared to set out for London and there complain of him before the High Commission Court, as a non-conformist. Attempting to mount his horse, he was seized with spasmodic pains and severe rebukes of conscience. He was carried into his house, and died in a few hours.

An event or two more, of less sad and different results, follow. During the continuance of Mr. Higginson in Leicester, a Doctor in divinity, prebendary in a Cathedral and chaplain to his Majesty, resided there, though he seldom delivered a sermon. The latter minister was far from cherishing a brotherly disposition towards the former, either in faith or forms. He saw, that whenever he himself discoursed from the pulpit, the multitude had gone after the Puritan. Such preference grievously wounded his spirit, and he declared, that the Town should be cleared of so popular a rival. But having thus committed himself to the public, he fell into a trying dilemma. He was nominated by the sheriff, three months beforehand, to preach at the Assize. The honor, so proffered, he could not well decline, but the preparation to discharge the duty of it, he could not make to his own satisfaction. The time, within a fortnight, had already expired, when he spoke of his anxiety, and expressed his fear to friends, that he should fail in writing a suitable discourse. They urged him to try again, but if he could not succeed, to call on Mr. Higginson, who was always ready, as a substitute. He did what he could, but without avail, till the very night before the Court assembled. Then, with emotions of mortification more easily imagined than described, he sent his wife to lady Cave, who desired Mr. Higginson to stand in his stead. The man, on whom he so loathfully depended, met his proposal kindly, and complied with his request, to the great acceptance of the large audience. But the end was not yet. After the particulars of the whole case were noised abroad, the public lost their respect for the Doctor so much, that he felt constrained to leave the place. In the meanwhile, their estimation of Mr. Higginson was greatly increased. Verily, the pit, prepared for the innocent, became the receptacle of its maker.

As Leicester was accounted a place generally favorable to Puritanism, many "courtiers, lords and gentlemen" agreed on a plan for tarnishing its good name, by degrading themselves. Accordingly they visited it, invited the mayor and aldermen to partake of a collation, and prevailed on them to drink so many healths on their knees, that they were intoxicated. This disgraceful scene became the topic of common conversation. Mr. Higginson, believing that the offence came within the Scripture injunction, "Them that sin before all, rebuke before all, that others may fear," felt it his duty to deliver a public discourse. This he did in the presence of the Mayor and Aldermen, from a text, which was the basis of his remarks on the sinfulness of drinking healths and drunkenness, and particularly so in magistrates, whose obligation was to punish it in others under their authority. He applied the subject by admonishing them to repent of the scandal, thus committed. The reproof was variously taken. They who lightly esteemed the yoke of Christianity, were much displeased, and denounced it as impudence instead of faithfulness. Of this class were some of the men implicated in the fault. Others, who had so fallen, made ingenuous confessions of their offence. Many more, who counted divine command far above human deception and resentment, approved the sermon. No ill effects appeared to come on the preacher.

After this, Mr. Higginson was selected by the Mayor and Aldermen of Leicester, to be their city preacher. But aware that he could not, consistently with his belief, coincide with all the requisitions of such a trust, he recommended to them John Angel, a worthy conformist. Several valuable livings were, also, offered him, which he declined for a similar reason. A clear conscience with him, was worth more than all earthly preferments.

While a conformist, he was often engaged in preaching visitation, assize and funeral sermons. Then and afterwards, he frequently took part in public and private fasts, and many resorted to him for the solution of their conscientious scruples. He did much service in teaching scholars, who were to enter, or who came from the University. Among them were Drs. Seaman and Brian, and Messrs. Richardson and John Howe, all of Leicestershire, who were eminent preachers, and expressed their obligations to him. When contributions were made for Protestant exiles from Bohemia and the Palatinate, he was among the most active to obtain them. Thus doing whatever his hands found to do, for the temporal and spiritual benefit of all, who came within the sphere of his action, his exertions, in that quarter, were soon to be curtailed and prevented.

Bishop Laud, having resolved to cut short all indulgence to Puritan preaching, entered, with a more vigorous hand, 1628, on the accomplishment of his purpose. He received complaints against Mr. Higginson, who, consequently, expected pursuivants, every moment, to take him before the High Commission Court, from which he looked for nothing less than perpetual imprisonment. Though we have no particular minutes to show how or when he was subjected to inflictions of law, yet his own assertion, on a subsequent occasion, assures us, that he "suffered much for non-conformity in his native land."

Influenced by strong faith, that Providence intended this country as an asylum for the persecuted Puritans, Mr. Higginson issued, before his embarkation, an able and eloquent publication.[1] This was entitled, "Generall Considerations for the Plantation in New England, with an answer to several objections." Its sound discretion and elevated motives recommend, that its leading thoughts should receive a passing notice. The considerations follow. First. It would be for the prosperity of the church in general, to have the Gospel planted on these shores, and would "raise a bulwark against the kingdom of Antichrist, which the Jesuits labor to rear up in all places of the world." Second. There was cause to fear, that God purposed to judge England, and to conclude that he had prepared the Colony as a refuge for his people. Third. England had an excess of poor population. Fourth. Emigrants hither would avoid the temptations before them, at home, from extravagance in living and dishonesty in business. Fifth. The literary and theological schools were expensive and corrupted. Sixth. Why should the poor starve, when there was land enough here for their support. Seventh. It is a noble work to help build up an infant church. Eighth. If any, possessed of wealth, take part in such an enterprise, they will give an example of self-denial, encourage emigration and the pious to pray for the prosperity of the settlement.

From these premises, Mr. Higginson proceeds to offer objections and answer them. First. "It will be a great wrong to our owne church and country to take away the best people." Reply. But a small proportion of the most exemplary will leave the kingdom. Whoever of them go, will have opportunity for greater usefulness. Second. Though we have long feared judgments, yet we are safe. Reply. So thought the churches of the Palatinate, Rochelle, etc. Their delay to flee and their ruin should be a warning. Third.

---

[1] Though some have doubted whether this was his, Hutchinson declares it to be from his pen. Its subject was similar to that of the Planter's Plea, by White, and of the Path Way, by Smith.

We have enough at home. Reply. We are like to have as good fare there in time, with the advantage of greater preparation for death and larger treasure in heaven. Fourth. We may perish or calamities come upon us. Reply. We should discharge duty and trust in God's Providence. Fifth. What right have we to the land of the Indians? Reply. A plague has swept off the most of them. What remain, welcome us. There is more than enough for them and the emigrants. Sixth. We should not send the best of our ministers and magistrates. Reply. If great things be attempted by weak hands, the result will be accordingly. Seventh. Other plantations have failed. Reply. Their want of success may be traced to lack of religious motives and proper instruments. The head which dictated, and the heart which deeply sympathized with these opinions and sentiments, were of no ordinary texture. Indeed, for the occupation of our soil, Mr. Higginson offered ingenious and forcible reasons. Great was the moral power, that enabled him and his associates to determine, that they would tear themselves from home and kindred, and embark for the inhospitable coast of a distant and unsubdued wilderness.

Probably referring to the treatise, a synopsis of which has been just presented, the Election Sermon of John Higginson, 1663, has the following passage:

"It is now 35 years since, I well remember, in the year 28,[1] that one of the first ministers, that came over into this wilderness, giving some account of his grounds, in a great assembly of many thousands at Leicester in Old England, he mentioned this as one, the mercy of the Patent, and the largeness of the Patent, from the royal authority of England, for the people here to choose their own magistrates, and to admit unto freedom such as they should think meet, and that religion was the principal end of this Plantation in his Majesty's royal intention and the adventurers' free possession."

So inclined, Mr. Higginson intended an extrication of himself and family from their afflictions, by a proposal to embark for Massachusetts, and consecrate his energies to the mission of dispensing the Gospel to the colonists and natives around them. In the transactions of the Company, who settled this territory, under March 23, 1629, we find the following record, literally and substantially. Information was given, by letters from Isaac Johnson, the husband of Lady Arbella, "that one Mr. Higginson, of Leicester, an able minister, proffers to go to our plantation, who, being approved for a reverend, grave minister, fit for our present occasions, it was thought by these present, to entreat Mr. John Humfrey to ride presently to Leicester, and if Mr. Higginson may conveniently be had to go this present voyage, that he should deal with him. First, if his remove from thence may be without scandal to that people, and approved by the consent of some of the best affected among them, with the approbation of Mr. Hildersham, of Ashley " de la Zouch ; secondly, he may leave his wife

---

[1] Likely in March, 1628–9.

and family till Bartholomew, so that they may be better accommodated with a passage, or not, as he prefers.

We are informed, that the persons, authorized to communicate with Higginson on this subject, were acquainted with his continual expectation of officers to apprehend him. Being more in the merry than sorrowful mood, they concluded to render such knowledge a source of final diversion, by letting him and his family suppose, that they were servants of the law. There may have been circumstances, unknown to us, which excuse a stratagem of this kind, but, as a general consideration, it is often injurious, and seldom the source of so much good as evil. The messengers knocked loudly at the door, and called aloud, "Where is Mr. Higginson? We must speak with him." His wife, greatly alarmed, as they might have thought, ran to his study, and entreated that he would secrete himself. He replied, "No, I will go down and speak to them, and the will of the Lord be done." They were admitted. Entering the hall, they approached him in a rough manner, and presented him with papers, saying, "Sir, we come from London; our business is to carry you thither, as you may see by these papers."

Mrs. Higginson, believing that her worst fears were about to be realized, exclaimed, "I thought so," and immediately began to weep. Her husband, however, soon indicated by his looks, that there was no cause for sorrow. The documents, so much dreaded as the messages of evil, were a copy of the Massachusetts Charter, and an invitation of the Company for him to be one of their efficient agents on the distant soil, to carry out their difficult enterprise. He welcomed his guests, conversed on the terms of contract, and other matters connected with the subject of momentous concerns. In view of this application, he first looked to God for direction, and then took counsel with his friends. Of these, Mr. Hildersham, who had long and severely suffered for endeavors to promote reformation in the National Church, said, "That were he himself a younger man, and under his care and call, he should think he had a plain invitation of heaven unto the voyage." Accordingly, he made up his mind, under the proffered conditions, to devote himself and his all again to the cause of philanthropy and religion in the new world. His resolve gave an impulse to many of like spirit, that they would do likewise.

After a few days, being the 8th of April, Mr. Higginson, and another, Samuel Skelton, of like motive, purpose, profession and trials, make the following contract:

"Mr. Francis Higgeson and Mr. Samuel Skelton, intended ministers for this plantacon, and it being thought meete to consider of their entertainment, who, expressing their willingness, together, also, with Mr. Francis Bright, being now present to doe their endeavour in their places of the ministerie, as well in preaching, catechisinge, as also in teaching or causing to be taught the Companys servants and their children, as also the salvages and their children, whereby to their vttermost to further the maine end of this plantacon, being by the assistance of Almighty God, the convertion of the salvages; the propositions and agreements concluded on with Mr. Francis Bright the second of February last, were reciprocallie accepted of by Mr. Francis Higgeson and Mr. Samuel Skelton, who are in euery respect to haue the like conditions as Mr. Bright hath, only whereas Mr. Higgeson hath eight children, it is intended that £10 more yearly shalbe allowed him towarde their chardges. And it is agreed, that the increase to be improved of all their grounds during the first three years, shalbe att the Companies disposeinge, who are to find their dyet during that tyme; and £10 more to Mr. Higgeson towards his present fitting him and his for the voyage.

FRANCIS HIGGESON,
SAMUEL SKELTON.

Further, though it was not mentioned in the agreement, but forgotten, Mr. Higgeson was promised "a man seruant to take care and look to his things, and to catch him fish and foule, and provide other things needfull, and, also, two maid seruants to look to his family."

The subsequent agreement of Mr. Higginson, includes some of the preceding items, and others of such interest, as to justify a condensed view of the whole.

He was allowed £30 to buy apparel and other articles for the voyage, and £10 more for books, and a free passage for himself, wife and children, and furniture. His salary for each of three years, commencing from his arrival at Naumkeag, was to be £30, a house and land, firewood and diet. The dwelling and appurtenances were to be a parsonage for the use of himself and successors in the ministry. At the expiration of three years, he was to have 100 acres of land assigned to him, and of seven years, 100 acres more. Towards the support of his household, he was to have the milk of two cows, and half the increase of their calves; the other half, with the cows, the Company were to receive at the end of three years. In case of his decease, his wife, while remaining his widow, and his children, if the former and the latter continued in the plantation, were to be supported at the public expense. Should he not like to dwell longer in the colony, than the period agreed on, there was to be no charge for a passage back for himself and family.

A letter is dated April 17, by the Governor and Deputy of the Company, and directed to Mr. Endicott at Naumkeag. It mentions the spiritual care, which had been taken for the settlement. "And for the propagating of the Gospel, is the thing we do profess above all, to be our aim in settling this Plantation. We have been careful to make plentiful provision of godly ministers, by whose faithful preaching, godly conversation, and exemplary life, we trust not only those of our own nation will be built up in the knowledge of God, but, also, the Indians may, in God's appointed time, be reduced to the obedience of the Gospel of Christ." The writers, having spoken of Mr. Skelton, as the instrument of religious benefit to Mr. Endicott, proceed to remark, "Another is Mr. Higgenson, a grave man and of worthy commendations. He cometh in the Talbot." They observe, in reference to these two and Mr. Bright, engaged in the same mission, "We pray you accommodate them all with necessaries as well as you may; and in convenient time let there be houses built them according to the agreement we have made with them." They state concerning them, that there is a prospect of harmony in their views and ministrations, which will be promoted by impartiality of the Government towards them and all others; that the manner and degree of their preaching to the colonists and natives, are left to their own discretion; and that, for their exertions to be duly appreciated, they must be fitly honored. They propose, that should these three ministers be unable to agree, which one of them should be located at Charlestown, it should be decided by lot, and whoever was so designated, should dwell there with his family.

Under the date of April 30,[1] the Massachusetts Company meet as a General Court in London, and attend to the choice of the Colonial Rulers. On this matter, their language follows.— "That thirteen of such as shall be reputed the most wise, honest, expert and discreet persons, resident upon the said Plantation, shall have the sole managing and ordering of the government and our affairs there, who, to the best of their judgments, are to endeavor so to settle the same, as may make most to the glory of God, the furtherance and advancement of this hopeful Plantation, the comfort, encouragement and future benefit of us and others, the beginners of this, so hopeful a work." Of the persons, so described in their qualifications and duties, was Mr. Higginson with his clerical brethren, Bright and Skelton. The first thought of having ministers among advisers to the chief magistrate, may seem inexpedient to the perception of modern usage. But when we reflect, that the chief purpose of the settlement was to have a Commonwealth, in which religion should be the paramount object, we at once discern the propriety of such an appointment. As the measures of legislation, so the legislators.

The oath[2] of office prepared and sent over for Mr. Higginson and his associates, is of the subsequent tenor. "You swear to be faithful and loyal to our Sovereign Lord, the King's Majesty, and to his heirs and successors. You shall, from time to time, give your best advice and council for supporting and maintaining the Commonwealth and Corporation of the Governor and Company of the Massachusetts Bay, in New England; not sparing for love nor dread, for favor nor meed, but according to the statutes and ordinances, made and to be made by virtue of the Charter of the said Company, shall effectually assist the Governor, or his Deputy and Council of the said Company, in executing the said statutes and ordinances; having no singular regard to yourself in derogation of the Commonwealth of the same. All these premises you shall hold and truly keep to your power, so long as you shall

---

[1] The fact of electing the members of the Government for the Colony, is mentioned in the letter of the preceding 17th, in the same month, to Endicott.

[2] This is mentioned, as being forwarded, by a letter of the Company begun to be dated May 28, and closed June 3.

continue in the place or office of one of the said Council. So help you God."

Prior to Mr. Higginson's having a proposition from the Company to engage in their service, his mind had been much exercised with regard to the critical situation of the kingdom, and it imbibed the strong impression, that the calamities of war would soon come on his countrymen. This led him to compose a discourse from the warning of our Saviour, Luke 21c. 20, 21 vs. "When you see Jerusalem compassed with armies, then flee to the mountains." Having decided to forsake the soil of his fathers and sojourn in a strange land, he concluded to adopt what he had so written, as his farewell sermon. In the presence of a large assembly, he did so, representing the sins of England, as the cause, which would bring on her such sufferings, in which Leicester would be a great sharer for its own transgressions. This prediction was remembered, by those who heard it, when the civil war prevailed between Charles I. and his opponents, and particularly when he and his forces stormed Leicester, 1645; took it, after a hard assault; captured immense spoil; made 1500 prisoners, and killed 1100 people in the streets. When Mr. Higginson had closed his discourse, he thanked the magistrates and others of the city for the kindness, which they had shown to him and his ministrations. He related to them his purpose of going to New England, and that the great object of settling there was the promotion of religion.— He expressed his hopes, that the Colony was divinely intended as an assylum for the non-conformists, from the storms coming upon the nation, and where they might have the free enjoyment of the reformation, for which they had prayed and labored. He concluded this extraordinary meeting, by an affectionate petition for the welfare of the King, the Church and State, and particularly of Leicester, the place of very many incidents, the most impressive and interesting in his life. When he and his family set out for London, the streets were filled with people, who, with loud prayers and cries, bid him farewell.

On April 25, Mr. Higginson sails in the Talbot from Gravesend. This vessel was of 300 tons, 19 guns, and 30 men, commanded by Thomas Beecher. She "carried about 100 planters, 6 goats, 5 great pieces of ordnance, with meal, oatmeal, peas and all manner of munition of provision for the plantation for a twelve month." She was one of three ships, fitted out at the same time with emigrants and supplies for the colony. She reached no further than Cowes by the 5th of May. Here, Mr. Higginson remarks, "I and my wife and daughter Mary, and two maids, and some others with us, obtained leave of the master of the ship to go ashore and refresh us, and to wash our linens."

On the 6th, "betime in the morning, the shallop was sent from the ship to fetch us to Yarmouth," being eight miles from Cowes; "but the water proved rough, and our women desired to be set on shore three miles short of Yarmouth, and so went on foot by land, and lodged at Yarmouth that night." Here they were detained. On the 10th, being Sabbath, "we kept the ship, where I preached in the morning; and in the afternoon, was entreated to preach at

Yarmouth, where Mr. Meare and Captain Borley entertained us very kindly, and earnestly desired to be satisfied of our safe arrival in New England, and of the state of the country." The following day, the Talbot, accompanied by the Lyon's Whelp, sailed with a fair wind. On the 12th, "We came as far as the Land's End, and so left our dear native soil of England behind us."

Cotton Mather informs us, that on this occasion, Mr. Higginson called up his children and other passengers to the stern of the ship, that they might give a parting look to the land of their nativity; and that he gave utterance to the emotions of his heart, as follows: "We will not say, as the Separatists are wont to say at their leaving of England, Farewell, Babylon! Farewell, Rome! But we will say, Farewell, dear England! Farewell, the Church of God in England, and all the Christian friends there! We do not go to New England, as separatists from the Church of England; though we cannot but separate from the corruptions in it. But we go to practice the positive part of church reformation, and propagate the Gospel in America." And so he concluded with a fervent prayer for the King, and Church and State, in England, and for the presence and blessing of God with themselves in their present undertaking for New England.

Johnson puts a question and gives its answer,

> "What golden gaine made Higginson remove,
> From fertile soyle to wildernesse of rocks?
> 'Twas Christ's rich pearle stir'd up thee toil to love,
> For him to feed in wildernesse his flocks."

Hard indeed must have been the separation of Mr. Higginson and family, from the country of their birth, education, home and most precious associations. But, encouraged by the promises of christian faith, that whether successful or not, in their pilgrimage to a new country, the blessing of heaven would be their portion, they bowed in submission to their lot, and heartily responded to the petition,—let the will of the Most High be done.

Having attended to the services of worship on the Sabbath of the 17th, as usual, Mr. Higginson relates, that two of his children, Samuel and Mary, were taken sick with the "small pox and purples together, which was brought into the ship by one Mr. Browne, who was sick of the same at Gravesend, whom it pleased God to make the first occasion of bringing that contagious sickness among us, wherewith many were after afflicted." On the 19th, Mr. Higginson's daughter Mary died, an event of sore affliction to her parents, and "terror to all the rest, as being the beginning of a contagious disease and mortality." On Thursday, 21st, in view of their anxiety and trial, a season of fasting and humiliation was observed. Messrs. Higginson and Ralph Smith performed the services. The former notes, "I heard some of the mariners say, they thought this was the first sea fast, that ever was kept, and that they never heard of the like performed at sea before." Tuesday, June 2, as the ship was delayed in her progress by contrary winds, some of the men sick with the scurvy and others with the small pox, he took part in another similar and solemn occasion. With the varied impressions of ocean scenes, made upon a mind of disciplined taste, which had never before witnessed them, Mr. Higginson notices the appearance of hostile vessels, the whale and other tenants of the deep, storms, floating ice, bank fogs, the death of a profane sailor, and of another child, sea funerals and the exhilarating sight of land. He observes, "We received instruction and delight in beholding the wonders of the Lord in the deep waters."

On the 26th, he writes, "By noon we were within three leagues of Cape Ann, and as we sailed along the coast, we saw every hill and dale, and every island full of gay woods and high trees. The nearer we came to the shore, the more flowers in abundance, sometimes scattered abroad, sometimes joined in sheets nine or ten yards long, which we supposed to be brought from the low meadows by the tide. Now what with fine woods and green trees by land, and these yellow flowers painting the sea, made us all desirous to see our new paradise of New England, where we saw much forerunning signals of fertility afar off." Thus welcomed to his intended residence by attractions of early summer's scenery, he and his fellow passengers were to experience a sudden but temporary disappointment. Having approached the entrance of Naumkeag harbor at dark, they tacked about for sea room.— About 4 o'clock, next afternoon, they reached the place which they left the evening before, and on the point of entering the desired haven, a squall, attended with rain, thunder and lightning, drove them back. Fearing to try the passage again, as night drew on, they made for Cape Ann. The subsequent day, being the 28th, and the Sabbath, was religiously kept there. As Governor Endicott saw the colors of the Talbot on Saturday, he then sent a shallop with two men to pilot her. But as these were blown out with her, they attended worship at the Cape. By their assistance, as Mr. Higginson remarks, and "God's blessing, we passed the curious and difficult entrance into the spacious harbor of Naumkeag. And, as we passed along, it was wonderful to behold so many islands replenished with thick wood and high trees and many fair green pastures." He proceeds, "We rested that night with glad and thankful hearts, that God had put an end to our long and tedious journey.

The next morning, 30th, the Governor came aboard and bade us kindly welcome, and invited me and my wife to come on shore and take our lodging in his house, which we did accordingly." One of his reflections on the voyage, gives us this extract: "We had a pious and Christian-like passage; for I suppose passengers shall seldom find a company of more religious, honest and kind seamen than we had. We constantly served God morning and evening, by reading and expounding a chapter, singing and prayer. And the Sabbath was solemnly kept by adding to the former, preaching twice and catechising. Besides, the master and his company used every night to set their eight and twelve o'clock watches with singing a psalm and prayer, that was not read out of a book."

Thus closes the journal of graphic descriptions, which Mr. Higginson gave of scenes, new to his experience and deeply impressed on his memory. Like the acts, which record the journeyings of Apostles to their places of Gospel labor, so this document tracks the course of its author to the spot of like sacred occupation.

At this point, it becomes us, in view of impressions, generally entertained, that Higginson and his company were separatists from the national Church, when leaving England, to enquire how the matter was, and how it stood on his arrival at Naumkeag. It is readily brought to mind, what his own language was, on bidding adieu to the kingdom, at Land's End. He then emphatically declared, that he and others with him, had not come out and renounced all communion with such an establishment. The fact was, that they were classed amongst church Puritans, who still continued to acknowledge her as a true Church, but to desire and endeavor, that the errors of doctrine and form, which had gradually crept into her sacred enclosure, might be speedily excluded. This was all consistent with his being denied the use of his parish pulpit and its revenue, because, while he could have coincided with some of the requisitions, there were others with which he could not, and still retain his integrity, as a man of truth and righteousness. It is evident, that the Company in whose service he was engaged, entertained views similar to his own. They were jealous, lest Ralph Smith, who came in the small fleet, which brought over Higginson and Skelton, should be too independent in his ideas and preferences, as to ecclesiastical polity. And so it turned out. Smith, soon after reaching our shores, went and preached for the Congregational church of Plymouth. But how was it at Naumkeag when the Talbot cast anchor in its waters? On the preceding May 11th, Endicott wrote to Bradford, a prominent member of the Plymouth church. He then stated, that through information of Dr. Samuel Fuller, who came to attend the sick, he had altered his opinion relative to its principles of government, and that he heartily agreed with them. This and several other events in the course of the year, show, that on the arrival of Higginson and his colleagues, he found the majority of the people at Naumkeag decided Congregationalists, while Roger Conant and the old planters probably remained Episcopalians. With matters so situated, and a mode of independent discipline in spiritual concerns, far more mild than they had realized, Higginson and Skelton appear to have soon harmonized, as the most practical, useful, and consistent with their sympathy and judgment. That they did so alter their position, is evident from the rupture between them and the Messrs. Browns, of which there will be occasion to speak more particularly.

Not long after Mr. Higginson entered on the round of his mission, the Council, of which he was a member, were convened at Salem. A prominent object of their session, was to have every settler sign the laws of the Colony. Among those called together, was Thomas Morton, of Mount Wollaston, who declined to subscribe his name. He was a stanch advocate for Episcopacy, and kept himself aloof from compliance with the orders of Government. These authorities sent messengers to apprehend him; but he eluded their search though they brought away what goods he left on the premises.

Near this time, Messrs. Higginson, Skelton, and Bright, settled the question, who of them should be stationed at Charlestown. The decision for this appears to have fallen on Mr. Bright, who had become the spiritual shepherd of the colonists in that place. Thus the territory, which John Oldham and his Episcopal friends were endeavoring to secure for themselves, as included in the grant to Robert Georges, was purposely occupied, as a part of the Massachusetts patent.

A letter from the Company, dated in London, May 28, and closed at Gravesend, June 3. and directed to Endicott, Higginson and others, reached its destination in a few weeks after the latter landed at Naumkeag. It gives several interesting orders. It requires that steps be taken to satisfy Indian claims to the territory; that an overseer be appointed for each family, so that servants therein, who were sent over at the charge of the Company, may be duly employed and so pay such expense; that a house of correction be built for the confinement of offenders; that, at the desire of Rev. John White, favor be shown to some emigrants from Dorset and Somerset; that the new settlers be not allowed to cultivate tobacco, except in small quantities for sickness; that none but "ancient men" be permitted to take it, and they do it privately; that the old planters be persuaded to discontinue the raising of such an article; that all the people be occupied in some useful employment, and no idle person be allowed to live with them, as a means "to prevent a world of disorders and many grievous sins and sinners."

That they might aid to secure the great design of the plantation, the leading men of Salem gave directions for the duties of July 20th, appointed by the Governor as a season of fasting and prayer. Charles Gott, in a letter to Governor Bradford, expressed himself as follows. "The former part of the day being spent in praise and teaching, the latter was spent about the election. The persons thought on, were demanded concerning their callings. They acknowledged there was a two fold calling, the one inward calling, when the Lord moved the heart of a man to take that calling upon him, and filled him with gifts for the same. The second was from the people, when a company of believers are joined together in covenant, to walk together in all the ways of God, every member is to have a free voice of their officers. These two servants clearing all things by their answers, we saw no reason but that we might freely give our voices for their election after this trial. Their choice was after this manner, every fit member wrote in a note his name whom the Lord moved him to think was fit for a pastor, and so likewise, whom they would have for a teacher. So the most voice was for Mr. Skelton to be pastor, and Mr. Higginson to be teacher, and they accepting the choice, Mr. Higginson, with three or four more of the gravest members of the church, laid their hands on Mr. Skelton, using prayers therewith. This being done, then there was imposition of hands on Mr. Higginson." The writer proceeds to state, that Elders and Deacons were named, but their ordination was deferred "to see if it pleased God to send us more able men over." Thus once more consecrated to the oversight of souls amid new scenes and relations, with strong desires and expectations to pursue his course unmolested, the occasion must have been associated in the experience of Mr. Higginson, as well as that of his colleague, with the soul's highest and holiest affections.

Near this date, troubles arose, which must have exceedingly tried the feelings of Mr. Higginson and his friends, as well as those of the individuals, whose sincere opinions placed them in the attitude of opponents. That the case may appear, as described by one of the cotemporaries, the subsequent passage is given from Morton's Memorial.

"Some of the passengers, that came over at the same time, observing that the ministers did not all use the book of Common prayer, and that they did administer baptism and the Lord's supper without the ceremonies, and that they professed also to use discipline in the Congregation against scandalous persons, by a personal application of the word of God as the case might require, and that some that were scandalous were denied admission into the Church, they begun to raise some trouble. Of these Mr. Samuel Browne and his brother were the chief, the one being a lawyer and the other a merchant." These "gathered a Company together in a place distinct from the public assembly, and there sundry times the Book of Common Prayer was read unto such as resorted thither. The Governor, Mr. Endicot, taking notice of the disturbance, that began to grow amongst the people by this means, convened the two brothers before him. They accused the ministers as departing from the orders of the Church of England, that they were separatists, and would be Anabaptists, etc., but for themselves, they would hold to the orders of the Church of England. The ministers answered for themselves. They were neither separatists nor Anabaptists; they did not separate from the Church of England, nor from the ordinances of God there, but only from the corruptions and disorders there; and that they came away from the common prayer and ceremonies and had suffered much for their non-conformity in their native Land, and therefore being in a place where they might have their liberty, they neither could nor would use them, because they judged the impositions of these things to be sinful corruption in the worship of God. The Governor and Council and the generality of the people did well approve of the ministers answer."

Though the denial here of being separatists, i. e. denunciators of the Episcopal Church, as though it were false in its principles and ordinances, was correct, as the deniers understood and used the term; yet they appear, as previously expressed, to have carried out their plan of reformation, as they believed it, more fully since their residence at Salem, than they did while in England. Such an advance they did not deny.

About August 1, the Government here, of whom was Mr. Higginson, write to the Company, who held their sessions in London, relative to their sad disagreement with the Messrs. Brownes, on the subject of Church order. The latter, also, forwarded a justification of their tenets and stand to the same authorities. The Governor had said, "that New England was no place for them," and he soon ordered them to embark for their native kingdom. This was a hard case for the Messrs. Brownes. Still it is evident, that, with the views and feelings of the two parties, while they remained together under the same jurisdiction, they would not attain to the object, for which the Colony was settled. Necessity demanded a separation, and that the chief of one or the other, should depart. So existing, it must have severely tried the good of both sides, who sought the welfare of the Plantation, and who knew, that contention must diminish its strength and retard its progress.

On the 6th, according to appointment, Mr. Higginson and his colleague take part in the services of the occasion. They are much interested in the adoption of the platform of rule, covenant and articles of faith, and the organization of their church. On this subject the Memorial of Morton thus speaks. Mr. Higginson "was desired to draw up a confession of faith and covenant in Scripture language, which, being done, was agreed upon. And because they foresaw, that this wilderness might be looked upon as a place of liberty; and therefore might, in due time, be troubled with erroneous spirits, therefore they did put in one article in the confession of faith on purpose, about the duty and power of the Magistrate in matters of religion. Thirty copies of the aforesaid confession of faith and covenant, being written out for the use of thirty persons, who were to begin the work." When the designated time arrived, "it was kept as a day of Fasting and Prayer, in which after the sermons and prayers of the two ministers, in the end of the day, the aforesaid confession of faith and covenant being solemnly read, the forenamed persons did solemnly profess their consent thereunto; and then proceeded to the ordaining of Mr. Skelton pastor, and Mr. Higginson teacher of the church there. Mr. Bradford, the Governor of Plymouth, and some others with him, coming by sea, were hindered by cross winds, that they could not be there at the beginning of the day, but they came into the Assembly afterward and gave them the right hand of fellowship, wishing all prosperity and a blessed success unto such good beginnings." Between this account and that of Mr. Gott, there is an apparent discrepancy. He relates, that the pastor and teacher were set apart to their offices on the 20th ultimo, and that because the agents concerned in this consecration, preferred to wait for an increase of emigrants so that a better selection might be made for the other officers, these were merely nominated and the ordination of them or others, who might come, was put off to the first Thursday of August. Being one of the prominent candidates to constitute the Church, he would be more likely to be correct in his communication, made on the 30th of the previous month, than Morton. The probability is, that events transpired as the former stated they already had or were to, and that the rest of the solemnities occurred according to the account of the latter.

The Covenant and Confession, so drawn up by Mr. Higginson, were adopted, for substance, 1658, at the Savoy by the Congregational Churches of England. Thus the spiritual provision he made for his own flock, became that of many others in his native country, after a remarkable revolution in favor of the very principles, for which he was excluded from his parish, and driven, as an exile, to a distant clime.

Among the incidents of thrilling interest to Mr. Higginson and the rest of his church, at their being gathered, was that in relation to Edward Gibbons. Scottow informs us, that this young man had associated with the inhabitants of Merry Mount, and that, however not vicious, he had little taste for Puritan Society; but that, having his curiosity greatly excited with reference to the formation of the church at Salem, he determined to be present. Continuing the narrative, the same author says as to the subject of his notice, "At which convention, the testimony, which the Lord of all the earth bore unto it, is wonderfully memorable, by a saving work upon a gentleman of quality, who afterwards was the chieftain and flower of New England's Militia, and an eminent instrument both in Church and Commonwealth." Gibbons would have united with the Salem Church immediately, but Mr. Higginson and his colleague, who were much pleased with the relation he gave of himself, advised that he should defer his wish for a season.

As another contribution to the information and pleasure of many in his native land, deeply interested in the civil, but especially in the spiritual welfare of the Colony, Mr. Higginson sends them a description[1] of its soil, climate, location, productions, natives and condition. While he represents the plantation in words, which express his attachment for it, as the home of his adoption and the object of his ardent hopes, he does not fail to be impartial in the confession of its disadvantages. Though some, influenced by his statements to emigrate hither, complained that they found less favorable realities, than they anticipated, still the integrity of his character forbids the suspicion, that his motives were in any manner deceitful. On this very subject, he observes, "The idle proverb is, *travellers may lie by authority*. Yet I may say of myself, as once Nehemiah did in another case, *shall such a man as I lie?*" He proceeds in his relation. He says, that they have a brick-kiln under way; the soil is very fertile and the Governor had planted a vineyard. He gives an account of the wild beasts around them; of the multitudes of fish and fowl. Speaking of the lights for their evenings, he specifies the oil from their fishery, and adds, that pitch pine slits serve them for a like purpose, as a custom derived from the Indians. He adduces objections to an abode here; as the winter is of greater severity than in England, the mosquitos troublesome, the rattlesnake poisonous, the want of more emigrants of worthy character, and a larger quantity of live stock. He adverts to his health, as being quite infirm prior to his embarkation, but much improved since his arrival. He attributes so favorable a change to the prevalent atmosphere; "for a sup of New England's air is better than a whole draught of Old England's ale." He informs us, that on their coming ashore at Salem, they found there about ten houses, and a respectable one

---

[1] This appears to have been sent from Salem by its author, some day of September.

"newly built for the Governor," and abundance of corn planted, which was in good condition; that they brought about 200 passengers, who had united with the old planters, in "one body politic," and that the number just named, still remained, though one hundred had located themselves at Charlestown, and that they had ordnance for fortification, sufficient to "keep out a potent adversary."

While Mr. Higginson dwelt on the concerns of the English with pleasant sympathies, his heart was also drawn to the remnant of the aborigines. He makes a few observations. "For their governors, they have kings, which they call Sagamores, some greater and some less, according to the number of their subjects. The greater Sagamores about us cannot make above three hundred men, and other less Sagamores have not above fifteen subjects, and others near about us but two. Their subjects, about twelve years since, were swept away by a great and grievous plague, that was amongst them, so that there are very few left to inhabit the country." After giving a description of their physical appearance, armor, and domestic concerns, he adds, "They do generally profess to like well of our coming and planting here, partly because there is abundance of ground, that they cannot possess nor make use of, and partly because our being here will be a means both of relief to them when they want, and, also, a defence from their enemies, wherewith before this plantation began, they were often endangered. For their religion, they do worship two Gods, a good and an evil God. The good God they call Tantum, and their evil God, who they fear will do them hurt, they call Squantum. We use them kindly. They will come into our houses sometimes by half a dozen or half a score at a time. We purpose to learn their language as soon as we can, which will be a means to do them good."

Leaving these subjects, though far from being indifferent towards them, he proceeds to that more sacredly enshrined in his affections. "But that which is our greatest comfort and means of defence above all others, is, that we have here the true religion and holy ordinances of Almighty God amongst us. Thanks be to God, we have plenty of preaching and diligent catechising, with strict and careful exercise of good and commendable order to bring our people to christian conversation, which whilst we do, we doubt not but God will be with us!" Such a conclusion shows where Mr. Higginson lay the foundation of his hope, and that he had wisely learned the immutable principles, on which alone society can be prospered and immortality be blessed.

About this time, Mr. Higginson addresses a communication to his numerous friends in Leicester, part of whom were anxiously waiting for information from him, so that they might decide the important question whether they should follow his example, come over and cast in their lot with the colonists. It is probably the one, to which Scottow calls the attention of his readers. "A letter then from New England, and for a considerable time after, was venerated as a sacred script, or as the writing of some holy prophet. It was carried many miles, where divers came to hear it, and a multitude of pious souls through the whole nation, were in their spirits pressed to join in this work." Several of its items are as follow. Its author states, that the Colonists were expecting to be reinforced with sixty families with their ministers from Dorsetshire, many others with their pastor from Lincolnshire, and a large number of christians from London. He advises persons of Leicester, where he had been forbidden to continue his faithful labors, who intended to join him in his new abode, to be expeditious, as the first comers " speed best and have the priviledge of choosing places " of residence. He counsels the rich to send over poor families to the plantation, " where they may live as well, both for soul and body, as any where in the world." He remarks, that Isaac Johnson, the husband of Lady Arbella, and others had thus assisted pious emigrants to engage " in their work for a while, and then to live of themselves." He says that there are forty goats, as many cows, six or seven mares, and one horse at Naumkeag. More of such stock are desired and expected. He wishes emigrants to bring as many of them, and, also, of sheep, as possible. Carpenters are greatly needed. The passage from England hither was £5 a man, £3 a ton of goods, and £10 a horse. He corrects mistakes, which some of the settlers had made to their disappointment, lest others, intending to follow, should have similar experience. He wishes adventurers hither to bring " woolen and linen cloth, leather for shoes, carpenters' tools, iron and steel to make nails, and locks for houses and furniture for ploughs and carts, and glass for windows," and adds " other things, which were better for you to think of there, than to want them here." In the following paragraph, he refers to the abundance of fish, which have long since been scarce in the Naumkeag waters. "Whilst I was writing this letter, my wife brought me word, that fishers had caught 1600 bass at one draught, which if they were in England, were worth many a pound." This document sets before us some impressive features of society but recently organized. It shows the need of energies, virtuously applied, which hold no communion with luxury, in order that such a community should conquer its difficulties and be prospered.

Letters from the authorities at Salem, including Mr. Higginson, are read to the Company in London, September 19, concerning the differences between them and the Messrs. Brownes, who appear to have arrived so as to be present. The case is left to referees. Among these, chosen by the Brownes, is William Pynchon, and by the Company, John Winthrop. On the 29th, a question is discussed by the Company, whether letters, in their hands, from the Brownes to their friends, and supposed to contain charges against the leading men at Salem, should be detained. It is concluded, that part of such communications be opened, some be read in presence of a committee and the persons, to whom they were addressed, and others kept. A copy of the charges from the Colony, against the Brownes, is ordered for them, as they desired.

The Court of Assistants in London, on the 15th of October, agree, that the salaries of Messrs. Higginson, Skelton and Bright here, and other ministers, who may come hither under their direction, and, also, the charge of erecting needed houses of worship in the Colony, and all other public works upon the Plantation, shall be borne, for seven years, one-half by the joint stock of the Company and the other by the planters.

On the 16th of the same month, the Court address the following letter to Messrs. Higginson and Skelton.

"REVEREND FRIENDS—There are lately arrived here, (being sent from the Governor, Mr. Endicott, as men factious and evil conditioned,) John and Samuel Browne, being brethren, who since their arrival have raised rumours (as we hear) of divers scandalous and intemperate speeches, passed from one or both of you in your public sermons or prayers in New England, as also of some innovations attempted by you; we have reason to hope that their reports are but slanders; partly, for that your goodly and quiet conditions are well known to some of us; as also, for that these men, your accusers, seem to be imbittered against you and Capt. Endicott for injuries, which they conceive they have received from some of you there; yet for that we all know that the best advised may overshoot themselves, we have thought good to inform you of what we hear, that if you be innocent you may clear yourselves; or if otherwise, you may be entreated to look back on your miscarriage with repentance, or at least to take notice that we utterly disallow any such passages, and must and will order for the redress thereof as shall become us; but hoping, as we said, of your unblameableness herein, we desire that this only may testify to you and others, that we are tender of the least aspersion, which, either directly or obliquely, may be cast upon the State here, to whom we owe so much duty, and from whom we have received so much favour in the Plantation where you now reside. So with our love and due respect to your callings we rest

Your loving friends,

Richard Saltonstall, Isaac Johnson, Matt. Craddock, *Gov'r.*, John Goff, *Dep'y*, George Harwood, *Treas'r*, John Winthrop, Thomas Adams, Symond Whetcombe, William Vassal, William Pinchion, John Revell, Francis Webb."

A literal compliance with every portion of this communication, was no easy matter for men with the experience and principles of Messrs. Higginson and Skelton. In a new sphere of action, where the iron grasp of law could not be laid upon them for the utterance of opinions and the practice of ordinances, which they had declared and manifested at the cost of exclusion from office and prosecution of person, in England, it was not only natural, but they felt it their sacred duty to preach and pray so as not to approve of Crown oppression towards the Puritans, while they commended the royal favor in their Charter privileges. Thus actuated, they were aware, that the eyes of others, who honestly differed from them, were constantly and closely upon every step of their course, and who, expelled from a participation in the privileges of the Colony and sent back to the kindom, whence they came, would as honestly declare every thing, offensive to them in their clerical action, in no measured or commendable terms. So situated, they wished to raise no unnecessary storm nor uselessly expose themselves to reproof of friends or censure of opponents. They took counsel from the oracles of Inspiration and endeavored to follow the dictates of heavenly wisdom. Thus guided, they went forward in the line of obligation, as they sincerely interpreted it, regretting to interrupt the plans and cross the interests of others, who tried to arrest their progress.

As an event, the tidings of which must have been welcome to the ears and hearts of Mr. Higginson and his colleague, the General Court of the Company in London, on the 10th of February, 1630, agree on a settlement of the difficulties, relative to the Messrs. Brownes.

Though Mr. Higginson had written to many of his warm-hearted friends in England, as to his high hopes of confirmed health and active ministry, his experience was soon to be the reverse. Called to witness scenes of great sickness and suffering, among his parishioners, the first winter of his pilgrimage here, and about one hundred of them, including the Ruling Elder, Henry Haughton, laid low by the hand of death, he was made more familiar with his own weak hold on life. It is not unlikely, that, amid his exertions to instruct and console the diseased and dying, as well as his subjection to an unaccustomed severity of the cold season, the hectic attacked him, which was to close his earthly career.

Though strongly desirous to give a personal welcome to Governor Winthrop and his friends, who arrived in the Arbella, at Salem, June 12, he was unable to accompany Messrs. Endicott, Skelton, Leavit and Pierce, down the harbor, for so pleasant a purpose. Still, while wasting disease was bearing him away from temporal scenes, his heart throbbed in grateful harmony with the thanks, given to God around him, for the arrival of supplies to the destitute and distressed colonists. The last of his pulpit efforts, was soon after the arrival of Mr. Winthrop and other recent emigrants. His text was from Matthew xi. 7. "What went ye out into the wilderness to see?" The several heads of his discourse were, that the chief design of the Plantation was religion; that various trials were to be expected in a new country; that the settlers should give proof, that their hearts were in unison with the professed object of their emigration. Having thus finished the work, divinely assigned him, he waited for the close of his appointed time, with peaceful submission to the allotments of Providence. Confined to his bed, he was visited by the principal persons of the Colony, who regretted, that they were to be deprived of his society, instructions and coöperation in promoting the interests of Puritanism. They spoke of his previous sufferings and faithfulness for such a cause, and of his being honored by the Lord in aiding to lay the foundation of "Church-reformation in America." He answered, "I have been but an unprofitable servant. All my desire is to win Christ, and be found in him, not having my own righteousness." He expressed his strong belief, several times, that, however he should be called away, God would raise up others to carry on the work begun, and that many churches of Christ would flourish in the country. Speaking of his wife and eight children, who were the strongest bond, which held him to this world, he observed, that however he must leave them with but a small portion of this world's goods, still he committed them to the care of God, who, he doubted not, would graciously provide for their wants.

Thus conversing about his earthly concerns in the exhibition of motives and sympathies, which manifested his constant preparation for heavenly realities, he enjoyed spiritual communion with his friends. So letting the light of his example rest for good on all, who saw him, he peacefully slept in death in August, aged 43 years. Many, who highly esteemed him in life, attended the solemnities of his funeral and followed the remains, which had tenanted his active and departed spirit, to their long and last resting place.

Though gone from his people, they had so learned his worth in the short period of his sojourn among them, that the pleasant and beneficial recollection of his precepts and influence, were often in their minds. Refering to him and other worthies, who had sunk before the devastations of disease, while engaged in the cause of religious reform, Governor Winthrop wrote to his wife in England, "The lady Arbella is dead, and good Mr. Higginson and many others." Thus remembered, Mr. Higginson, as already intimated, was courteous and obliging, with talents of high order, well cultivated in literature, oratory and divinity. Johnson says of him, "A man indued with grace, apt to teach, mighty in the Scriptures, learned in the tongues, able to convince gainsayers." The spirit, so qualified, was fitted to take a prominent part in heaven's mysterious agencies, and gloriously realize the hopes of his earthly pilgrimage.

Before we leave the subject of this memoir, we will take a short notice of his family, whom he committed, in faith, to the protection of their covenant keeping God. His wife and children resided in Salem, for a period, how long not known, and experienced much kindness from the people there and the liberally disposed in other places. On the 26th of January, 1631, she wrote to Governor Winthrop a letter of thanks for "two kine and house and money in the hands of Mr. Coddington." This aid was probably, in part, compliance with the agreement between her husband and the Company, that she and her children should be supported by them, if he died, so long as they remained in the Colony, and, also, by the contribution of some principal colonists of ability and liberality. With regard to the latter assistance, Cotton Mather informs us, that it was given so that the widow and her family were comfortably situated. With our wishes so pleasantly gratified in their welfare, we follow them to New Haven. But when they went thither, or why, we are not told. They of course, would not be there sooner than 1638, when the place was settled by Theophilus Eaton and other prominent puritans. It is likely that this worthy gentleman was the means of their removal from Massachusetts, because he seems to have been a relative to them, perhaps her brother, from the facts, that one of the sons bore his christian name, and another, after her decease, went to live with him. But the time of her sojourn in the last town, must have been quite short. She appears to have died in the early part of 1640, survived by eight children. In this year, February 25, as she left no will, the Court of New Haven, with the consent of her eldest son, settle her estate and provide for her family, as follows. John, considering the charges of his education, is to have his father's books and £5 in bedding. Francis, the second son, and Timothy, the third, in view of their education also, are each to receive £20. Theophilus, however well educated, because of helpfulness to his mother and benefit to her property, is allowed £40. Samuel is assigned £40 and to live with Mr. Eaton for two years from the 1st of next March. He and Theophilus are granted "the lot with all the accommodations belonging thereto, equally divided betwixt them, for £50 of their portions." Anne, the daughter, is to have £40 with part of her mother's clothes, and "the remainder of the estate when the debts and other portions are paid." Charles is to receive £40, be an apprentice with Thomas Fugill, nine years from the March 1, who is to keep him at school one year or give him learning to such an amount. Neophytus, being with Mr. Hoff or Hough of Massachusetts, is to live with him till 21 years old, during which period Mr. Hough is to keep his £40 and then pay this sum to him. When the farm at Saugus is sold, the price is to be equally divided among the brothers.

As well known, John lived and died, an eminent minister, in Salem, 1708, aged 92. Francis finished his life at Kirby Steven, in Westmoreland, England, after a very useful ministry, 1670, in his fifty-fifth year. Timothy followed the seas and died a bachelor. Theophilus deceased at the age of 37, and left a son, Samuel, who became a physician. Samuel was captain of a man-of-war in the reign of Charles II., and afterwards commander of an East India ship, and died at the age of 44 years. Charles commanded a ship in the Jamaica trade, and deceased when 49 years old. Neophytus died at the age of 20 years. Some accounts state, that Anne was married to a Chatfield. There was a Mrs. Higginson living at Charlestown in 1669, but who she was more particularly, we have no facts to show. Thus we have succinctly traced the offspring of one among the worthiest founders of New England. We take our leave of him and them with the heartfelt aspiration, that our motives may be of the same high standard with his, and our last end illumined with the light, which rested on that of so eminent a benefactor.

This book should be returned to the Library on or before the last date stamped below.

A fine of five cents a day is incurred by retaining it beyond the specified time.

Please return promptly.

MAR 25 53 H

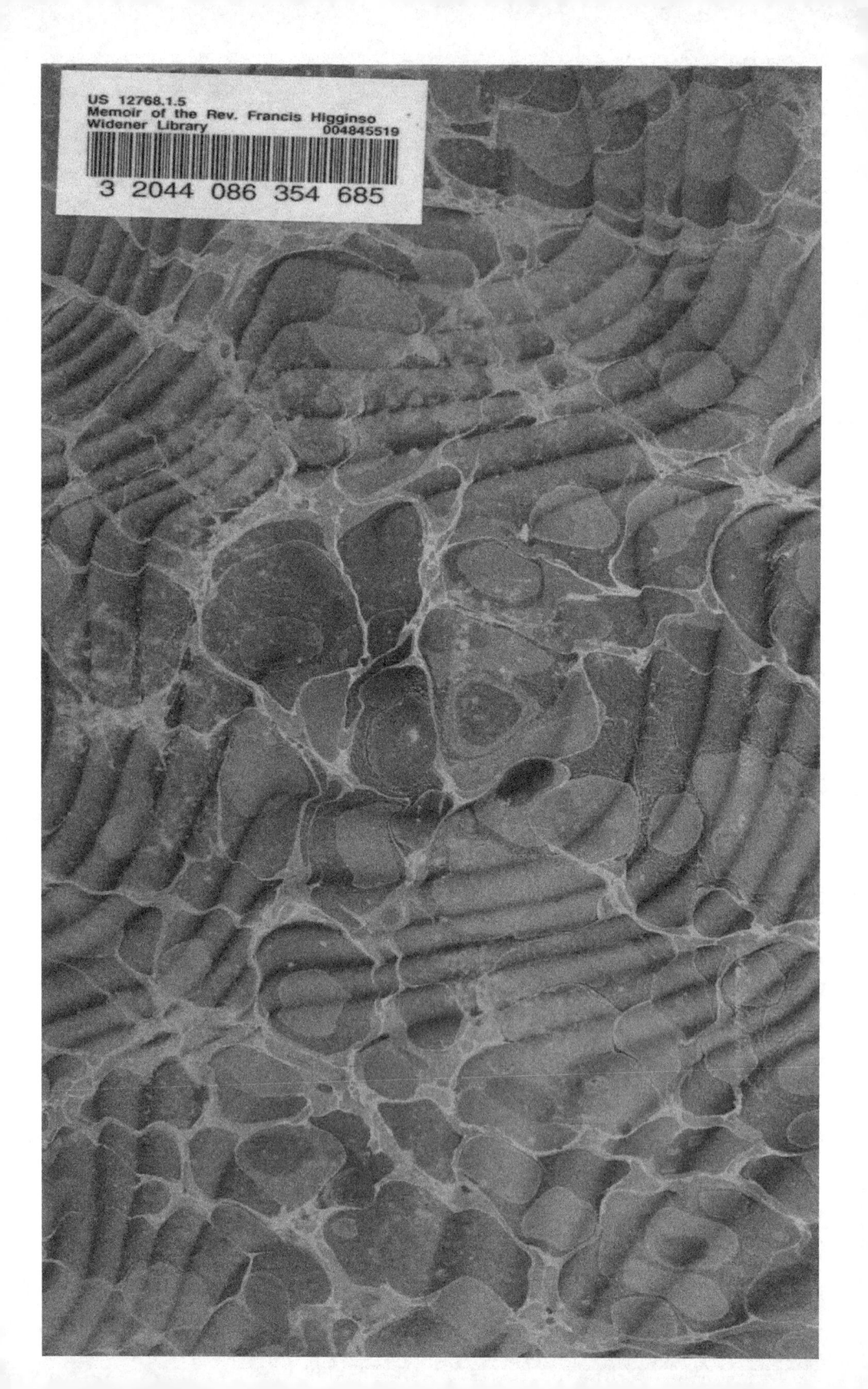

Check Out More Titles From HardPress Classics Series In this collection we are offering thousands of classic and hard to find books. This series spans a vast array of subjects – so you are bound to find something of interest to enjoy reading and learning about.

Subjects:
Architecture
Art
Biography & Autobiography
Body, Mind &Spirit
Children & Young Adult
Dramas
Education
Fiction
History
Language Arts & Disciplines
Law
Literary Collections
Music
Poetry
Psychology
Science
…and many more.

Visit us at www.hardpress.net

Im TheStory
personalised classic books

"Beautiful gift.. lovely finish.
My Niece loves it, so precious!"

Helen R Brumfieldon

★★★★★

JANE IN WONDERLAND
LEWIS CARROLL

UNIQUE GIFT

FOR KIDS, PARTNERS AND FRIENDS

Timeless books such as:

Kids

Alice in Wonderland · The Jungle Book · The Wonderful Wizard of Oz
Peter and Wendy · Robin Hood · The Prince and The Pauper
The Railway Children · Treasure Island · A Christmas Carol

Adults

Romeo and Juliet · Dracula

- **Highly** Customizable
- **Change** Books Title
- **Replace** Characters Names with yours
- **Upload** Photo it's inside page!
- **Add** Inscriptions

Visit
ImTheStory.com
and order yours today!

CPSIA information can be obtained
at www.ICGtesting.com
Printed in the USA
BVHW040107130819
555665BV00021B/3200/P